THE RIDER'S HANDBOOK

THE RIDER'S HANDBOOK

DIANA R. TUKE
Photographs by Donald Tuke

J. A. Allen
London & New York

First published 1977
by J. A. Allen & Co. Ltd
1 Lower Grosvenor Place
London SW1W 0EL
and in the USA
by J. A. Allen
Sporting Book Center
Canaan
N. Y. 12029
© J. A. Allen & Co. Ltd.

ISBN 085131 258 6

British Library Cataloguing in Publication Data

Diana R. Tuke
The Rider's Handbook
1. Horsemanship
I. Title
798'.23   SF309   77-30582

ISBN 0 85131 258 6

Printed in Great Britain by
Lewis Reprints, London and Tonbridge

Contents

1. Reasons for riding

There are many reasons why we ride – some do it for pure enjoyment; others because it is the thing to do; while for some it is the passport to freedom from some form of disablement or illness. Many ride for more than one reason, and each reason can be sub-divided.

To ride well, one must enjoy it; though those who enjoy it do not necessarily ride well! These latter riders get a great deal of pleasure, but never aspire to greater heights than just hacking quietly or having a weekly ride. The former on the other hand normally find that the better they become the more they wish to get out of their riding.

The second category ride just because it is the 'In thing'. They may or may not enjoy it, but would rather die than admit they did not. If they have the ability then they will enjoy it in the end as they become better riders. They will often find a fulfillment out of doing something well. Alas, these riders often have little or no feeling or real love of their horses, and even less understanding of their temperaments and needs – they are merely a means to an end. On the other hand the first group normally do care.

Lastly, we have those whose health can be greatly improved by riding - Riding for the Disabled in fact. Riding is one of the finest remedial exercises going, and but for riding many a disabled person would not be up on their feet and walking today! For this band of riders there is something far greater than just plain enjoyment to be gained. For them it opens the doors of a closed world and enables them to regain a great deal of their lost freedom and find a sense of real achievement – while on their horse they are equal to the next. To put into words quite what this feeling is, is extremely difficult, nevertheless, believe me it is very real, and being able to re-join one's fellows on equal – or, more or less equal, terms goes a long way towards helping such a rider have the will to regain their strength. These riders may require to take a little extra care and go a little slower than a fit rider, but nevertheless, their problems are really no different than those of fit riders who decide to take to the saddle in later life.

It is principally for the older rider that this booklet has been written, to start is not always easy, but once launched then progress and standard should not be any less obtainable than that of a rider say in their twenties or teens.

Some riders have ridden as small children then given up, while others have for some reason never had the chance or wish to ride. Why they wish to start in later life varies. For those who have never had the chance through lack of money, or having to work, it merely means they are fulfilling a life long dream and good luck to them. If a thing is worth doing then it is worth waiting for. In the case of those riders who have never had any desire to ride before, I have often found it is parents who, having married someone who does ride (father or mother, it works either way) then have children who inherit the riding parent's love of the game and ride too, leaving the non-riding parent out of everything. On the principle of if you can't beat them, join 'em, the non-riding parent decides to start and before long is often as keen, or keener and as good as the parent who has always done it. Another factor that brings parents into the riding game is when a pony is outgrown or the child who rides is away at school and the pony must be got fit for the holidays – the child expects the parents to do it – so they do!

In cases like these people hate to be made to look foolish while they are learning. Regrettably the riding part of a family will often merely laugh at the new recruit. Not wishing to make fools of themselves they try, often in vain, to get help from outside their families to buy their clothes and get their initial lessons. It is these people I aim to try and help, so that they may start with confidence and expectancy of the happiness to come.

2. Clothes and how they should fit

Once we have decided that we wish to start riding, then the next important hurdle to clear is that of getting ourselves suitably clothed. Now riding clothes are designed with a purpose in mind and are not a gimmick. Their object being to provide protection to the rider and enable him or her to ride as well as possible; besides of course, being neat and tidy – in short, workmanlike.

Admittedly most riders have at some time or other ridden perfectly happily in ordinary clothes, nevertheless, unless one has a hide like a rhinoceros, one will collect bruises that one will not forget in a hurry – bruises that are avoidable if we wear correct clothes that fit.

The habit of many riders to ride without a hard hat and in either jeans or trousers, is not to be encouraged and for a newcomer to the equestrian world, decidedly dangerous. Heads must have a hard hat to protect them and the legs require proper boots (long or short) and breeches or jodhpurs according to the riders preference. This is the minimum amount of clothes we can get away with. Besides these two main items a coat of some sort will also be required in winter.

Buying riding clothes is never easy, and for the newcomer one of the hardest hurdles to clear. If one does not know what to ask for, or how it should fit, then one is at the mercy of some shop assistant who may or may not know. They have a habit too, of making one feel a nit-wit – something no one need feel if they know beforehand what it is they require.

Each branch of riding has its own special requirements with regard to clothes; what you wear for one branch, will not necessarily be correct for another. In this chapter I am going to deal with each garment and how it should fit, and in a later one what you should wear for different occasions.

1. A workmanlike turn-out. A correctly fitting velvet cap; tweed jacket; collar and tie; breeches and long boots complete with blunt short necked spurs.

Hats – these must be hard and fit perfectly if they are to afford the protection and safety they should. Every rider must wear a hard hat for competition work and should also do so for ordinary riding and schooling.

A human head is a vulnerable object that must not be treated with contempt. A blow to the head can cause serious and often lasting brain damage – damage that can in most cases be avoided if we wear a suitable hard hat to protect it. Some people have thinner skulls than others, but how thick or thin one's head is is something no rider knows until it has been put to the test – if thin and unprotected, then it could be too late. Therefore do not be foolish, but be sensible and wise before not after the event – *Wear a hard hat.*

Inches	$19\frac{5}{8}$	$20\frac{1}{8}$	$20\frac{1}{2}$	$20\frac{7}{8}$	$21\frac{1}{4}$	$21\frac{5}{8}$	22	$22\frac{1}{2}$	$22\frac{7}{8}$	$23\frac{1}{4}$	$23\frac{5}{8}$	24
cms.	50	51	52	53	54	55	56	57	58	59	60	61
English Size	$6\frac{1}{8}$	$6\frac{1}{4}$	$6\frac{3}{8}$	$6\frac{1}{2}$	$6\frac{5}{8}$	$6\frac{3}{4}$	$6\frac{7}{8}$	7	$7\frac{1}{8}$	$7\frac{1}{4}$	$7\frac{3}{8}$	$7\frac{1}{2}$

When buying a hat for riding one must take into consideration the fact that no two rider's heads are quite the same shape. Heads are like eggs and vary in their shape in much the same way. Basically the head is slightly wider across the brow and tapers to the back. Few heads are completely round. To measure one's head pass a tape-measure round the brow and over the greatest part of the skull at the back, just above the ears. From this measurement the hatter will decide what size hat you require. Makes vary a bit so you may find a one-eighth variation in sizes from one make to another and one type to another. This applies mainly to those whose heads are border line cases for size. Some large hatters will measure your head by placing what reminds me of the 'Mad Hatter's' hat on one's head – this can be adjusted to each lump and bump and through a card placed in the top, produce a pattern to which the hat of your choosing can be altered to fit you. If one has an odd shaped head – a lump from an accident or something, then this is well worth the extra expense. Only good hatters use them.

A cheap hat for riding is no use, they are normally 'soft' and quickly lose their strength, which is after all their protection. Some too, even crack on coming into contact with the ground, these are useless. No, I am afraid whatever else one may save money on, one must not save it on one's hat – one's hat could be one's life.

To fit a hat correctly it must be put on square – *never* on the back of the head. Hair must be brushed back off the forehead and confined neatly by some means or other. Next the hat is placed with its front edge on the brow and the back is then gently, but firmly, pushed down over the back of the head till it fits snugly. A good fit should keep the hat on under all but the most exceptional circumstances.

Confining hair for a woman is a problem. If short and neat then I am a believer in wearing no net – some believe in nets however short the hair. My reason for this lies in the fact that a net causes the hat to tend to slip; without a net the hat can grip the hair and remains more firmly on the head come wind or hard riding. If a net is worn then try and get one that is not slippery

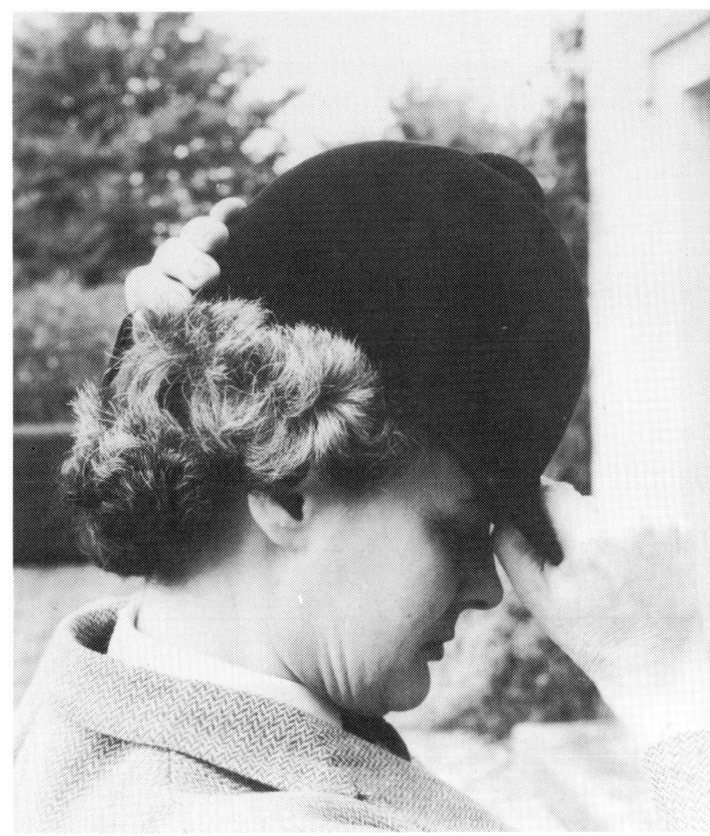

2. Putting on a cap so that it will fit firm and snugly and at the same time be in the correct position which is square.

and do not place it over the forehead but well back on the top. This allows the lining of the hat to grip the skin. Children with long hair can have it plaited or tied neatly in a bunch down their back. The habit of some women to wear a silk scarf under their hat is mad – a hat big enough to take such a scarf is far too big and therefore useless! Another pet abomination of mine is those riders who put their hats – mainly caps, on the backs of their heads with all their hair emerging round it like a pie crust frill – the hat is useless, even dangerous as it can never stay on.

Hats come in several forms. RIDING or HUNTING CAPS in velvet being the most useful and popular. These must be of good quality and made without a hard screw ventilator in the crown or a fixed brim. The brim must be so constructed as to break free on hard impact. Many children's and ladies' caps

3. Incorrect – this cap is useless even dangerous to the wearer.

are made so light as to be more or less useless in the event of a hard fall. For this reason I now wear a top quality man's cap – or as the trade call them 'Gent's'. These are made really for Masters of Hounds and Hunt Servants and are twice as strong as the ladies' caps. I changed when the hatter at one of London's oldest hatters decided it would be far safer for me to wear a gent's cap as the others are now not nearly so strong – the price was the same! Of all my riding clothes my caps are the one thing I do not save money on. It would be foolhardy to do so. To fit correctly a cap should come down over the back of the head so as to cover the weak spot at the base of the skull. When placed on a flat surface the cap should be shaped with an arch – the back and the front resting on the surface and the middle arching upwards. Those caps that lie flat and are circular in shape are a waste of money as they will never grip the sides of the head. To test that the back is the correct length – put the cap on and then bend the head back. If the cap lifts off the head, then the cap is too long at the back and does not fit. A cap like this will come off every time the rider's head goes back. Of all the riding headwear, caps are the safest for general riding.

Bowlers – these are brimmed hats made of stiffened felt. Like caps they have a draw string inside that enables the wearer to adjust the amount they come down on the head. *An inch must be given between the top of the head and the lining of the hat, regardless of type.* Incidently the small white bow is designed to indicate the back of the hat and not for adorning the forehead as I saw it out hunting last season on one lad!

Silk hats – these are tall hats for wear on formal occasions.

Crash skulls – these very strong shells, fitted with chin harness to hold them securely on the rider's head, are used for racing and eventing, and other cross-country riding where the rider is likely to have a hard fall. The shell is covered by a silk or nylon cover in a colour of the rider's choice and is made with a soft peak. Care must be taken to adjust all the harness and draw strings very carefully.

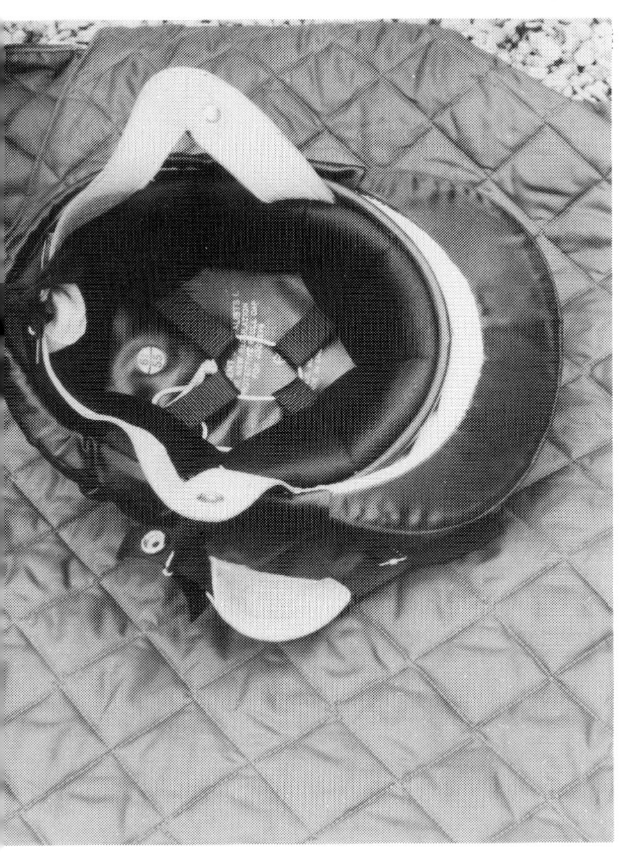

4. A crash skull showing safety harness and drawstring.

5. The same crash skull complete with nylon cover and with the chin harness fastened.

If a hat is too big and the next size down too small, then the difference can be adjusted by placing strips of thin foam inside the lining across the brow, and if necessary, across the back also. In a few cases the strips can be placed along the sides instead of the former. It depends on the shape of the rider's head. The hat must be snug fitting.

Harness, similar to that on crash skulls is now fitted to some caps, or sold loose to fit over the cap. These are only safe if adjusted correctly and the cap fits in the first place. Should the cap be too big, it can slip and get rammed either into the bridge of the nose, or worse still the back of the neck – highly dangerous in either case. So care is required when using this type of harness on a cap with a shaped back and fixed peak. Elastic is safer if a chin strap is required, though it will not stop a cap coming off in the event of a fall.*

Colours, except in the case of covers for crash skulls, are out of place in riding. Velvet caps – velveteen or cloth for the cheaper grades, can be black, blue or brown, other colours should be avoided. Bowlers come in black – the usual colour, or brown in a few cases. Grey being the summer wear of those on foot for special functions during shows etc. Silk hats are normally black for riding, with grey for special occasions during the summer.

So much for hats, we now come to BREECHES – these terminate at the calf; and JODHPURS – which continue down to the ankle encasing the calf.

The object of wearing breeches – worn with long boots, leggings or stockings (which will

* A British Standards Institute approved soft peaked safety cap is now available, thanks to the British Horse Society, and is to be recommended.

not protect the leg in the case of a fall should the horse step on one), or jodhpurs – worn with special short boots, is to give the rider a close feel of their horse and to be able to grip without the leg slipping. Too, they prevent bruising. Over the years the cut of breeches and jodhpurs has altered. In the last decade or so we have seen the coming of the slim fitting instead of the wide flair of pre-war days. This wide flair now looks very old-fashioned and so too does the pear shaped flair that came in in the early sixties. Nevertheless, the straight flair we have now-a-days can be carried too far and no one should wear their breeches or jodhpurs looking as if a quart has been forced into a pint pot. The modern cut, if not carried to extremes, can be smart and look very workmanlike. The main fault with these breeches and jodhpurs is that they are cut too short for the wearer. This

6. Nylon stretch jodhpurs worn with elastic-sided jodhpur boots. Note where the knee seam comes, in the groove below the knee.

makes the material – normally stretch nylon – follow every crease and crevice of the wearer's body like a second skin. Getting ready-made breeches and jodhpurs to fit is not always easy, but some firms might do a 'special order' for a few extra pounds. This means riders with long thin legs can get a pair to fit them, and also have the waist to fork measurement made that extra inch longer which enables them to fit comfortably without pulling.

The waistband must shape into one's waist with ease and not be pulled down excessively when one bends over. The waist to fork measurement must be long enough to prevent pulling between the legs. The seam that comes below the knee must fit snugly into the groove above the calf and below the knee joint – this seam keeps the leg of either breeches or jodhpurs down in their correct place. The calf must fit well so as to avoid excess wrinkling and afford some support to the leg. The ankle in the case of jodhpurs must fit so that there is no more than an inch clearance around the ankle. If the legs are too big the jodhpurs will ride up and wrinkle on the leg. Too tight, and the circulation of the legs will be impaired giving the rider cramp. Breeches and jodhpurs are reinforced where the greatest wear comes – inside the legs and sometimes with jodhpurs, around the ankle. These strappings can either be self strapping (the same material) or buckskin, a form of leather. Nylon material normally has self strapping. Breeches and jodhpurs can be made in several materials – cavalry twill being the accepted one in either wool, cotton or nylon stretch material. Colours range through from dark fawn to white. Pale fawn being the most suitable for ordinary riding. *Never* wear coloured or fancy breeches or jodhpurs, these are incorrect.

Boots – specially made for riding have shaped legs to fit the calf snugly in the case of long boots. Boots must be long enough to reach within half an inch of the bottom of the knee and the top should fit as close to the leg as possible. The heels on these boots have a specially shaped instep to prevent the stirrup iron getting caught. Leather used to be the only material in which long boots were made, and is still the best if one can afford them. Alas, they are very expensive. Rubber has for this reason come on the market and there are many good boots now available. Choose a boot with a firm leg and foot that does not feel too like a gumboot. Black boots are never wrong; brown can be worn for hacking and polo. Normally worn with breeches, boots can be worn over jodhpurs, in which case one's jodhpurs just become breeches – a very satisfactory economy. For children and those who prefer wearing jodhpurs as such, then special jodhpur boots are required that slip under the cuff of the jodhpur, fitting close to the ankle to give support. Elastic-sided boots are the most comfortable and give good support providing the elastic is sound and fits close to the ankle. Strapped boots are more bulky and do not give in the same way when one presses down one's heel to use the leg. Whichever pattern of boot is chosen the ankle part must be straight up and not, as in so many inferior boots, sloped to the rear. These latter boots merely cut into the front of the ankle and stand off behind the heel.

Coats – these are the next item on our shopping list. For ordinary hacking and exercising an anorak answers very well providing it is clean and fits. Cheap and warm they look perfectly acceptable. Nevertheless, for formal riding a proper coat is essential and everyone who intends either riding at a riding school or in public, should own one. Tweed jackets are correct wear for ordinary riding. These should be of closely woven tweed or suitable material and are made with sloping pockets. The skirt of the coat has a slight flair to enable it to lie neatly when the rider is mounted and the vent at the back is either single – up the centre, or double, giving a flap. Soft greens of a darkish hue or fawns toning to deeper brown are the most suitable colours. Black coats are cut either like a hacking jacket but with a single vent, or for more formal occasions, with swallow tails. These latter are worn with a silk hat. The former with either a velvet cap or bowler. For showing dark blue coats are often favoured by children and ladies, in which case the black cap is replaced by a navy blue one. A blue coat can be worn for hunting if dark enough. Velvet

7. Black coat worn with a black velvet cap and correctly tied hunting stock; breeches and long boots complete with spurs. The rider is carrying a hunting whip and is wearing string gloves.

collars also have their place on showing coats if the wearer cares for them, but they are strictly for showing and are out of place for anything else. If one can only have one coat, then buy a tweed one, they are always right. Far too many black coats get worn when they should not be.

Shirts – these require a collar and tie if worn with a tweed coat. Choose a shirt of a plain colour and soft hue that blends with one's coat. White is always correct if in doubt. For showing a collar and dark tie are the order of the day with a black or navy coat. White or pale blue shirts being in place with the latter. For hunting, showing, dressage and sometimes show jumping a hunting stock is often worn and for this a shirt with only a neckband is required.

Pullovers – these are either the 'V' necked sort, if worn over a shirt for extra warmth, under either a tweed or black coat; or POLO-NECKED if worn for either cross-country riding (eventing) or for hacking, in which case they are worn either on their own or under a tweed coat or anorak, but *never* under a black coat as we so often see nowadays. This is very wrong indeed. In warmer weather a sleeveless sweater can be worn in place of the 'V' necked long sleeved one, if desired.

Gloves – string or leather are necessary to afford grip, stop blistering and in winter, to help prevent one's fingers getting completely frozen. White gloves are correct for some occasions, but brown, fawn or yellow are usual. The fawn are very smart and if string gloves of the crochet type are bought, will last far longer than the ordinary yellow knitted string ones, as they do not show the dirt so easily, and wash for ever. Gloves must fit snugly – too loose and they will slip about on one's hands causing fumbling with the reins. I find youths' gloves are often quite large enough for a woman with regards to string gloves. Ladies' are often far too large once washed a time or two. Buy them as tight as you can to start with, especially string ones.

Hunting stocks – shaped ties that fold round the neck to give support in the case of a fall, are required if you decide to hunt or go in for competitive cross-country riding (in which case they are worn under one's sweater). Some dressage competitions also demand the wearing of a stock to be correct. Coloured ones with spots are only permissible for those who favour them for hacking, otherwise white is the only colour. Made of silk or pique (a stiff finely ribbed cotton that washes well and always looks fresh when well ironed), these stocks are normally shaped and have a slit on one side to allow the crossing of the stock behind the neck. Made up stocks are useless and only for 'the so-called' rider and never worn by a true horseman or woman. The following photographs show how a stock should be tied. A workmanlike effort can be achieved with a little care by even a newcomer to the art. A well tied stock looks very smart – a badly tied one ghastly. Sadly the latter are more common than the former.

Our riding clothes are now complete – not that we will require them all to start with, and if properly cared for will last for years. Wash those things that are washable; brush those that require it and have those that cannot be washed dry cleaned when necessary.

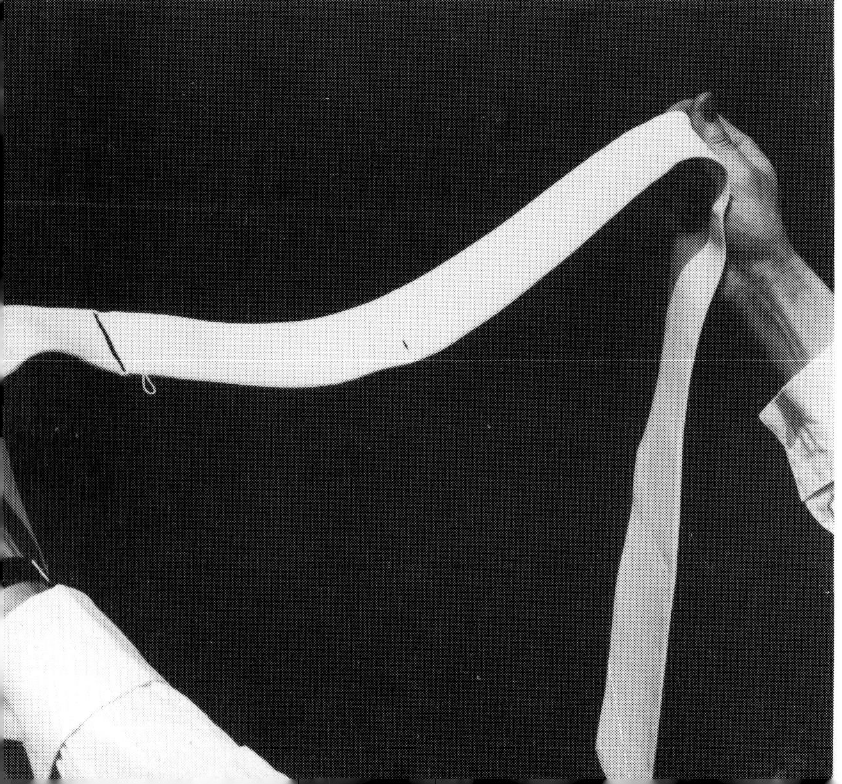

8. Showing the shape of the stock. Note the slot on the left-hand side and elastic loop for fastening to back stud or button, and central button hole for fastening to front stud or button on shirt.

9. Stock buttoned on to front of shirt neck-band.

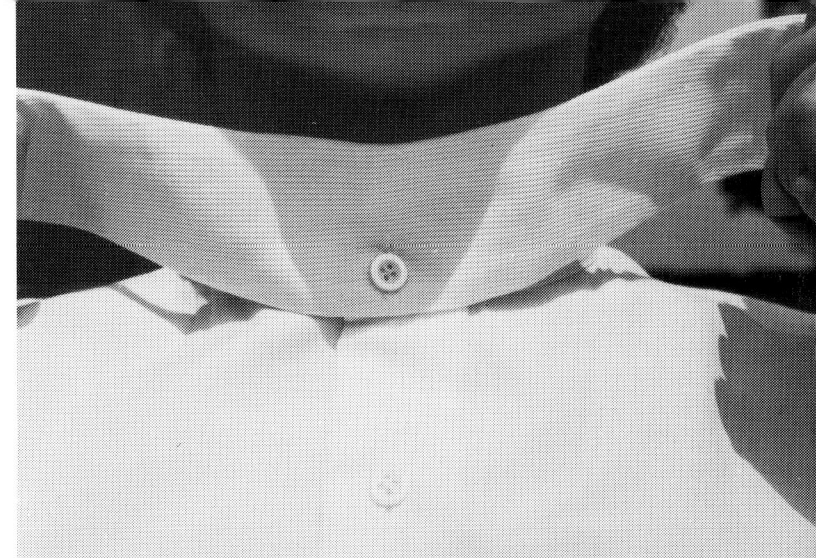

10. Next pass elastic button loop over back stud or button to anchor the stock to the back of the shirt; now pass the right hand end of the stock through the slot at the back.

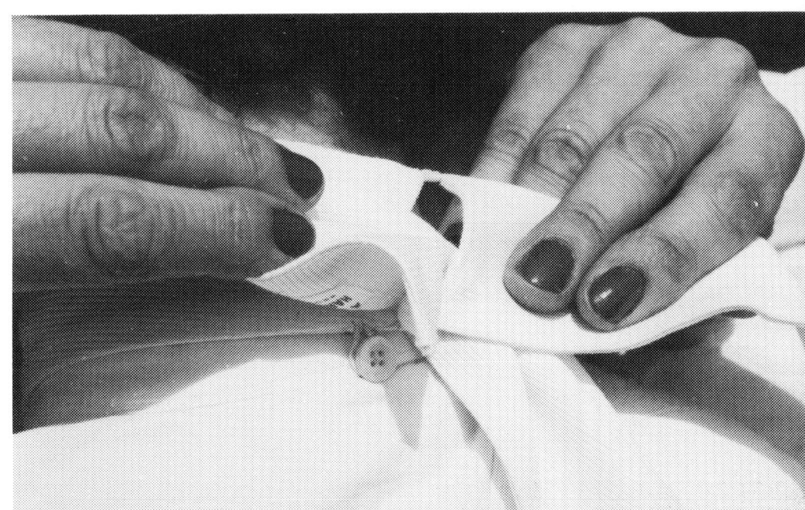

11. This allows the stock to cross at the back of the neck; next pull both ends evenly so that the stock fits snugly round the neck – the stock is for protection, so must be put on as closely as possible, while still allowing the wearer room to breathe and swallow.

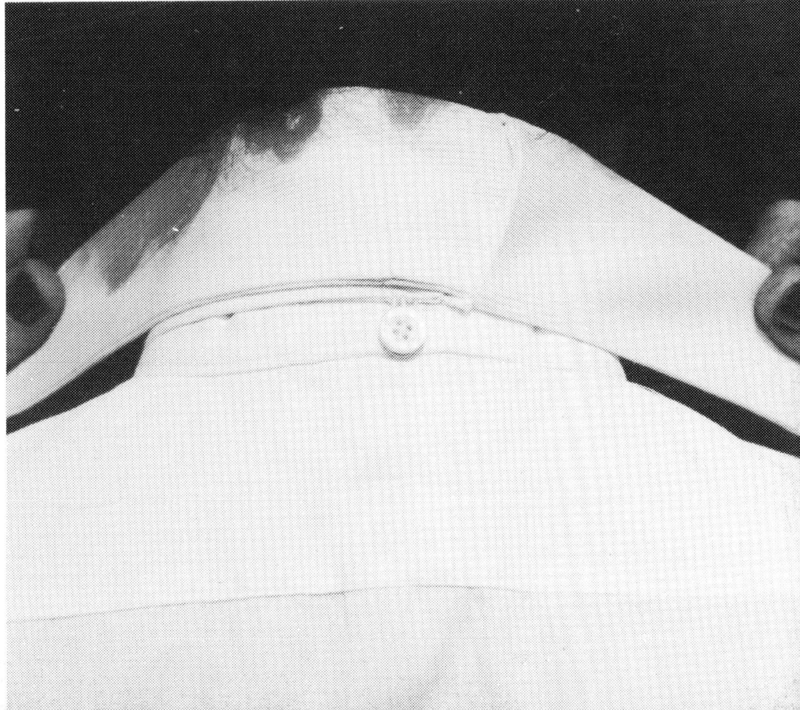

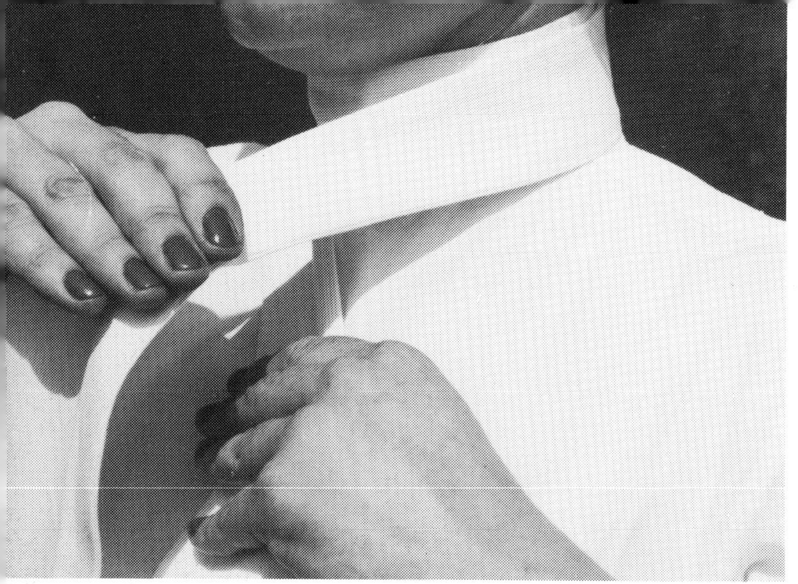

12. Now cross the left hand end of the stock over the right hand one so that they lie central over the front button.

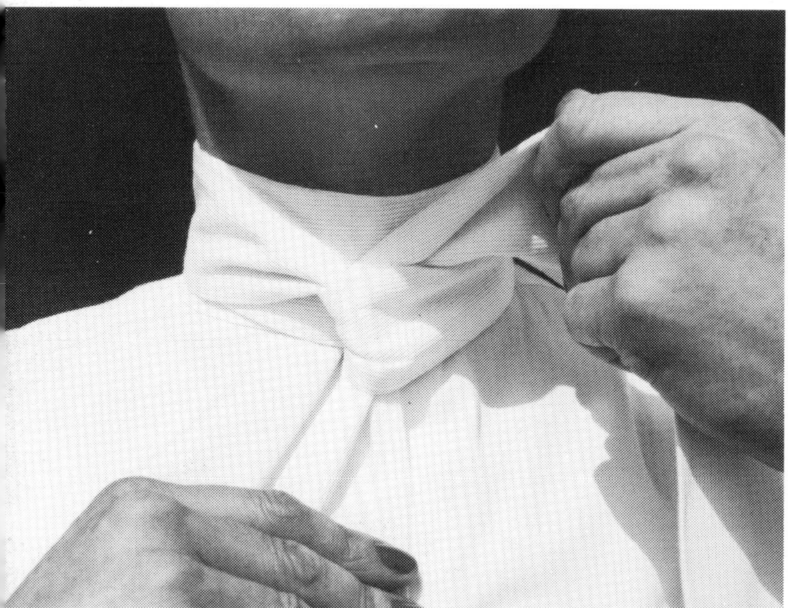

13. Then, taking the left hand end pass it up under the right to form a half knot.

14. Having pulled the knot firm, square off the top so that the top end lies down flat.

15. Now, holding the top end some
three inches from the knot with the
left hand, fold end up to lie flat
over the right shoulder.

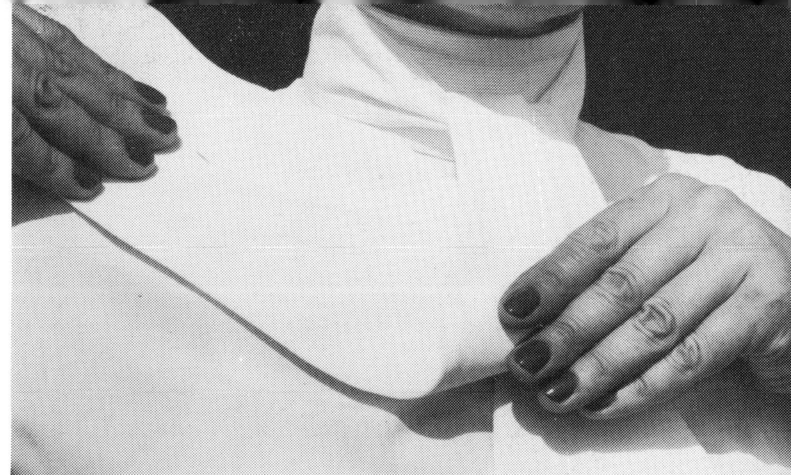

16. With care, now double the
bottom end up and pass it through
the loop made by the top end,
taking care not to crease the stock
in so doing.

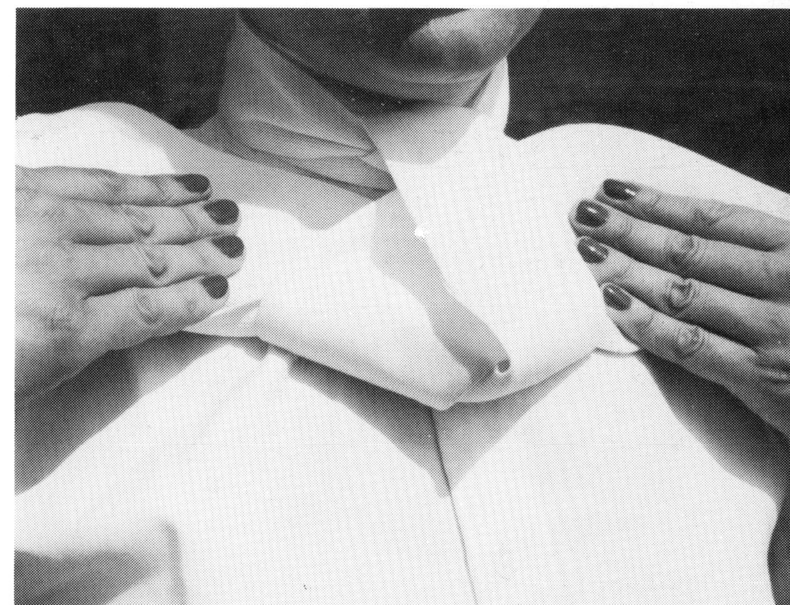

17. Now, gently but firmly take a
hold of both ends evenly and pull so
as to form a firm knot, square under
the wearer's chin.

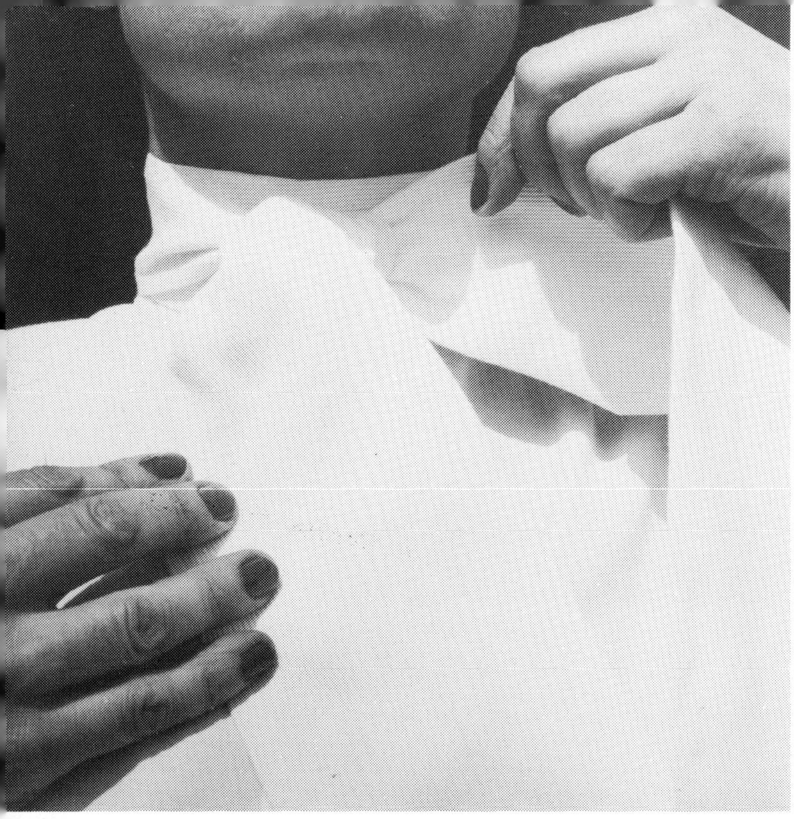

18. Having made sure the knot is square, fold the right hand end carefully down and across the knot at a slight angle so that it covers half the knot.

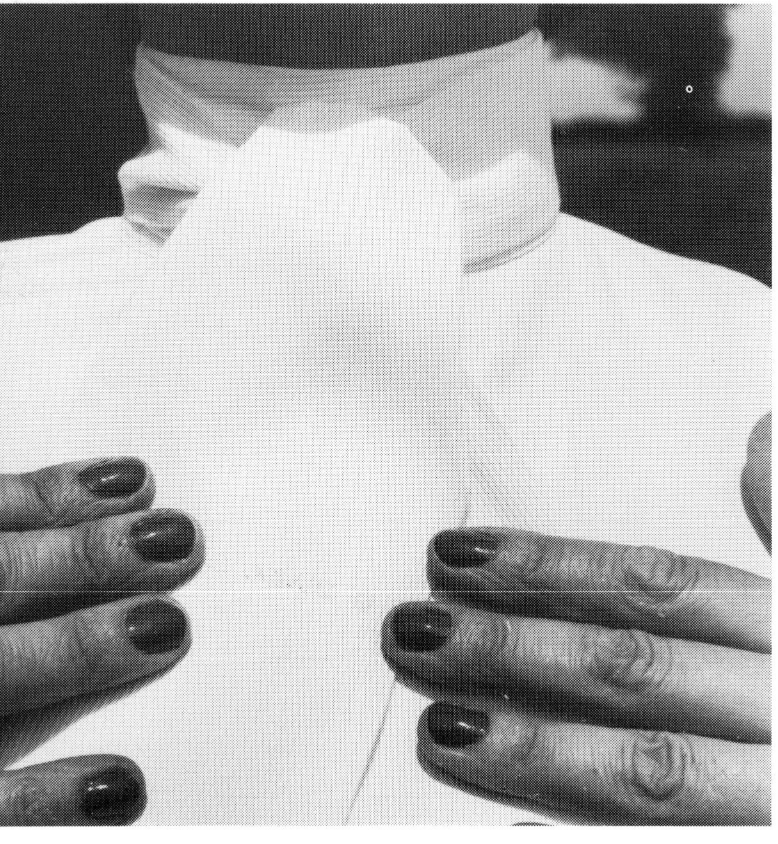

19. The lefthand end is now folded down in like manner to lie over the right and cover the rest of the knot – real perfection should bring the edges of both ends to meet at the top of the knot, otherwise the righthand end can overlap the left, providing it gives a really neat appearance.

20. Now, carefully place a hand under the stock and behind the front opening of the shirt, and with the other hand pass the pin of a simple stock pin – either plain or with a small emblem (mask, horse shoe or miniature whip) through both stock and shirt directly below the knot.

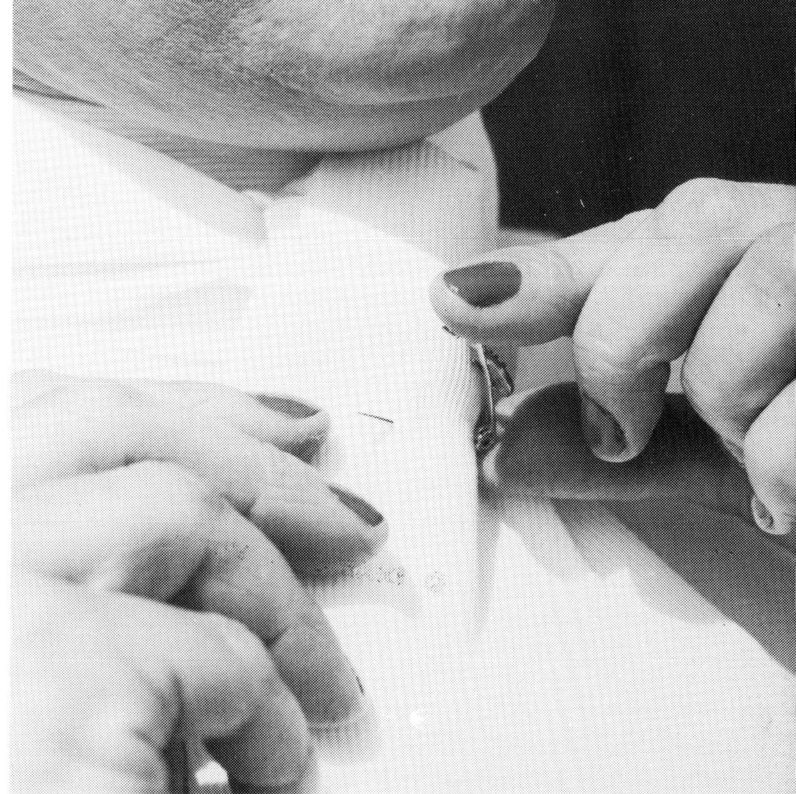

21. Once in place fasten and then adjust the top of the stock to ensure the knot is covered and stock neat and workmanlike.

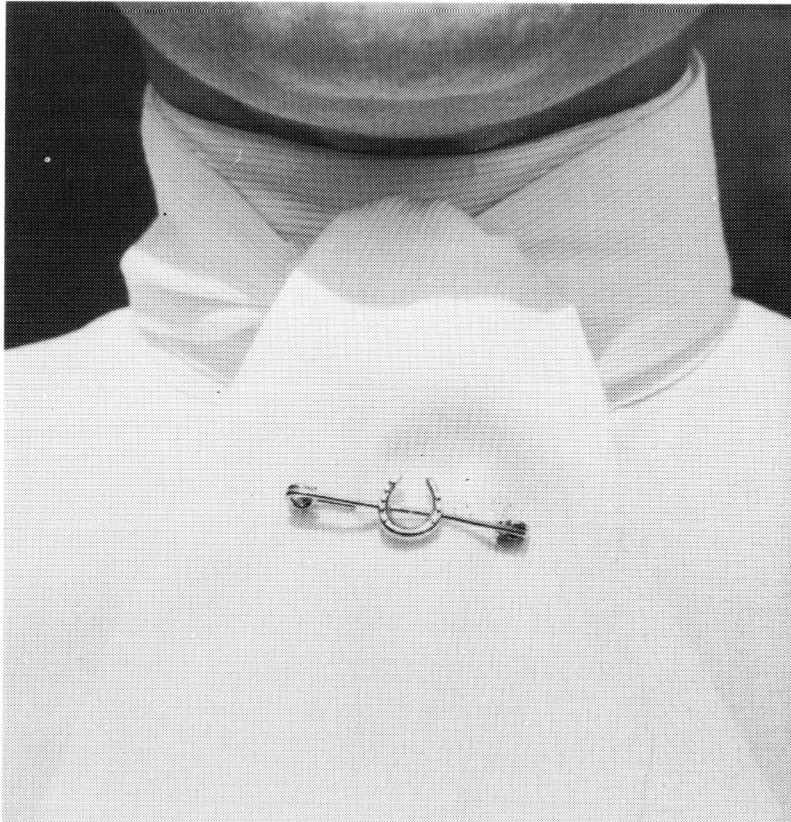

3. An introduction to riding

Your head and your heart keep up,
Your hands and your heels keep down,
Your knees close into your horse's side,
And your elbows close to your own.

Who wrote the above verse, or where I first heard it, I do not know, but I do know that it is very true. Every rider, or would be rider should know it off by heart and remember it at all times.

Riding is largely a matter of balance and being able to go with the horse's movement. At first this will be very difficult, but after a few rides the 'feel' of the horse will come. Once the rider has acquired this feel, even to a limited extent, the whole process of riding will become easier.

It is essential to try and sit correctly from the start. Failure to do so will only lead to bad habits – habits that become very hard to get rid of later on. An ordinary balanced seat is what every rider should aim at acquiring. This seat will give the rider good control and is later on easily adapted for different forms of riding should the rider wish to do more advanced riding like show-jumping or cross-country work. An efficient rider should have a seat that is independent of both the rider's hands (no relying on reins to maintain balance) and legs (the lower leg being free to apply the aids).

When a rider first starts to ride or resumes riding after a lapse of time, muscles will be brought into play that have not been used in ordinary life. For the older rider these muscles will take time to adjust to their new role. The big mistake so many people make is asking too much too quickly of their muscles – they become very sore, tired and strained by the unaccustomed efforts they have been called upon to perform. This leaves the rider very stiff and sore, and also far weaker in the saddle than need be. Never ride for more than twenty minutes to start with. Once the muscles have started to grow accustomed the rider can increase the time spent riding each day. Walk for the first week and then start trotting if the balance is good enough. But only for very short spells.

Exercises help a great deal in tuning up the muscles. It is rather like skiing, one has to prepare oneself before going off the deep end and trying to complete a whole ski run or in this case an hour's ride or more.

One exercise I have found extremely helpful to strengthen the calf muscles and help the ones used in one's back is merely knee bending.

22. An ordinary balanced seat is what every rider should aim at acquiring. The rider here is dressed in formal hacking clothes, and Galavant – a dark brown 15.1 hand Thoroughbred mare has an Eggbutt-sided jointed snaffle, with a drop-noseband and running martingale, and an all-purpose saddle complete with a sheepskin numnah.

23. Knee bending – stand with feet apart.

Stand with your feet apart and facing forwards.
Now gently bend them, all the time keeping the
back straight and the head up. One is in fact
adopting the position one uses on a horse but
there is no horse. Start by doing three or four
bends at a time, then as one feels it less, increase
it. Once one can bend a fair way start pushing
with the back downwards at the end of the fifth
bend. WARNING stop if it hurts, the object is
to strengthen not strain the muscles. Following
my accident I found this exercise helped me
regain the power in my back and legs, both of
which had been lost. I still do the exercise, and
if I know I am going to have to use my muscles
extra hard, like in an event, I do this exercise
every day in addition to my riding, in order to
strengthen my back and legs so that they can
cope. It looks a little odd, so do it when you are
on your own – it only takes a minute or two at a
time, so can easily be fitted in, however busy
one is.

Another way to help get the feel and acquire
an independent seat that does not rely on one's
reins and stirrups to maintain balance, is to
make a dummy horse on which to do exercises.
If one has some bales of either hay or straw
(wheat or oat, never barley) and possibly a sack
of corn, then one can make a very satisfactory
'horse' which will not walk off without
permission. The real horse too, is spared the
worry of a beginner trying to carry out
exercises, while the rider is given the feel of
sitting astride an object, and the leg muscles get
accustomed to being bent at an unusual angle.
Place two bales on their sides close together
and on the top of these place a third one flat.
This will give the average height rider enough
leg clearance off the ground. If one has a sack,
and one feels it more comfortable, then this can

24. Then, keeping the head up and the shoulders
back, bend the knees; pushing downwards from
one's back through one's knees to one's heels in
order to bring into play one's riding muscles.

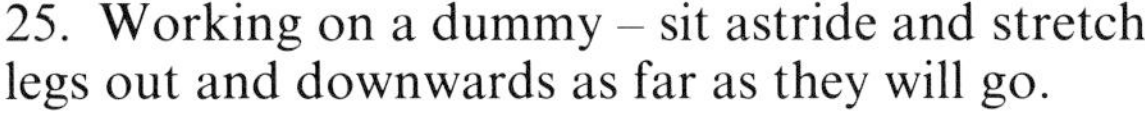

25. Working on a dummy – sit astride and stretch legs out and downwards as far as they will go.

26. Next bring your legs into the correct riding position with knees against the sack and bales.

be placed on top of the top bale to form a soft saddle. Now climb on top and sit in the centre stretching the legs down each side as far as possible. Having done this, bend the knees and bring them in close to the sides of the bale or sack just as if one was sitting on a saddle. The knee and toe should be in line and the heel pressed down. Try and maintain the legs in their correct position throughout the exercises. Do not swing them to the rear or poke them forward to maintain balance, one must grip, and move the body from the waist. Start by bending forward and then sitting up again. This stretches and supples the back muscles. As the days pass increase the number of bends – always going slowly to avoid strain. Other exercises which help include swinging the lower leg from the knee to and fro, to help give an independent lower leg to apply the aids.

Bending down to touch the toes using the hand on the side opposite to the toe – keep the leg correctly placed. Sit up straight and bend the trunk of the body round first one way and then the other.

How easy these exercises will be depends largely on the build of rider and the age. Thin and active and you will find the progress fairly fast compared with the heavily built with shorter legs. Long legs grip easier than the short plump sort, but both given the will can ride equally well if they wish.

Once the rider has become accustomed to the movement of the horse, these and more complicated exercises can be carried out on the move as well as at the stand still, they are in fact part of learning to ride. Wear a hard hat at all times, not only can one slide off the dummy, but it helps to get one's balance correct.

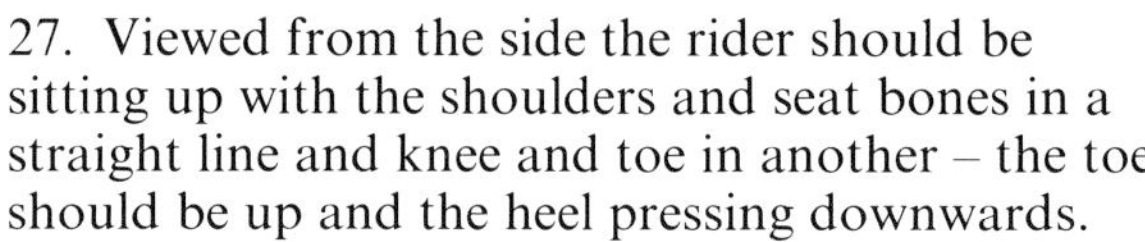

27. Viewed from the side the rider should be sitting up with the shoulders and seat bones in a straight line and knee and toe in another – the toe should be up and the heel pressing downwards.

28. Now while maintaining the correct leg position, bend forward.

29. Another useful exercise is to touch one's toes with the opposite hand, all the while maintaining the correct leg position.

The main thing to remember is that the older rider and the disabled one must not push the pace. Give one's muscles a chance and one stands as good an opportunity of becoming an efficient rider as a much younger person.

Whatever happens do not ever think you are looking a fool – the young can look just as foolish as an older rider, and in either case it is pure nonsense to worry over a trifle like that!

4. Where to learn

Having acquired the necessary riding clothes and tried to work up some of the muscles that will be required when riding commences, the time has come to start. The question is, how and where to start.

For those who already own horses or ponies then they will probably start at home. For the rest, well, if they have no friend with a suitable horse or large pony, then the only answer is to go to a good riding school. Many older riders seem reluctant to go to a riding school. This is wrong, schools should have and be willing to accept the older rider. During the holidays and at week-ends the children will be around, but during the term time the week days should be available for older riders to ride in peace.

One of the principal problems that face the older rider is that of nervousness. Unlike the young, they have lived long enough to realize accidents can happen, and therefore have a justified fear. A fear that if tackled sensibly and kindly can be removed by a good instructor fairly quickly once the confidence of the rider has been established.

Comfort on the part of the rider goes a long way to giving confidence. A good saddle of modern design is essential. A sprung tree with a dipped seat helps the rider to sit correctly from the start. This in itself is a boost for the ego. Those old, hard saddles that shoot the rider off the cantle (rear of saddle), merely strain the rider's back and make that of the unfortunate horse very sore. Reins too, should be the type that do not slip through the fingers too easily. Rubber covered or plaited are the best. Width should be considered too – wide ones are very hard to grip. Far better have narrow reins that the fingers curl round easily.

The horse chosen is equally important. Quiet

30. Incorrect – too short leathers; rider on the fork and pitched forward relying on the reins for balance, the true sense of which has been lost.

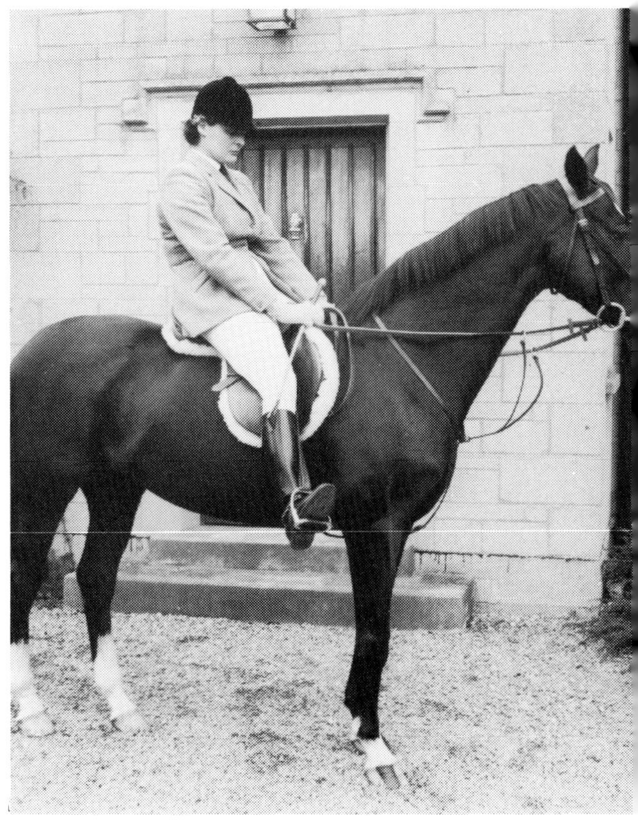

31. Incorrect – the other extreme; the rider's leathers are too long, the legs have shot forward and the whole weight of the rider is placed on the horse's loins – the weakest part of their back, the rider's balance has been lost too.

and kind, besides being long suffering, are the prime essentials in either horse or pony. A good shoulder and smooth paces come next. A rough ride never helps to encourage good riding. Do not choose too large a horse to start with, far better go for a strong, well made half-bred whose height does not feel too far from the ground. If over 15.2 hands, unless the rider is very tall, will, until the rider has suppled up, be far harder to mount and dismount. Providing the horse is well schooled and willing, the rider should find the first lessons not too tiring.

I do not propose to go into the actual riding in this handbook, as it would be far better for the rider to read one or two really good, easy to understand books. The British Horse Society's *Manual of Horsemastership* will prove invaluable and should be in every home. If the children already ride then no doubt there is already a copy in the house. *Riding* by Mrs V. D. S. Williams is another book which will help the rider understand how to sit correctly. Avoid if possible leaning forward and clutching at the reins, this merely makes the legs swing back and all balance is then lost. The lower leg must be kept straight down with the heel drawn back slightly. In this way balance is maintained even if the body goes forward with the movement of the horse.

Before going to a riding school it is essential to know something about the correct care of horses and ponies, otherwise the intending rider has no idea if the place is being well run or the horses and ponies fit to ride. *Horse by Horse*, a guide to equine care, covers the subject about as fully as any book can; and its companions, *Bit by Bit*, a guide to equine bits and bitting; and *Stitch by Stitch*, a guide to equine saddles and saddling, will provide a pattern by which the rider can judge if the school is worth attending.

The British Horse Society have an approved Riding School scheme and can let any would be rider have a list. This list is well worth acquiring. It is a waste of time and money to attend a bad school, and even, in some cases, dangerous. The saddles and bridles will be in poor repair – this leads to accidents that could and should be avoided, the horses and ponies, in a poor and overworked condition, being expected to work on too little food with their feet badly shod. Unfortunately there are too many schools whose standards do not come up to that required by law. Therefore be wise and ask the British Horse Society for their list.

A fit horse or pony should have a bright eye, a well covered body with a shine to its coat and be willing to work sensibly without getting tired. Its feet should be well shod with the shoes fitting correctly – too long feet and loose shoes only cause suffering to the horse and the risk of accidents to the rider.

5. Some do's and don'ts when riding

Do remember your head is a governing factor in your balance, if you let it go forwards or sideways without using your legs and back muscles to counteract the movement, you will follow it!

Don't if you find yourself falling stick out a hand or arm to save yourself (instinct makes one if one is not careful) as this is how you can break an arm. There is nothing to be ashamed of in falling, it merely pays to know how to fall correctly.

Do remember to try and tuck your head in as you go down and curl up like a hedgehog, going limp if possible at the last minute. Parachute jumpers land by rolling over like this.

Don't though decide you are falling long before you are. Many falls are quite unnecessary once you have gained your confidence and balance.

Do remember a good rider is one who can move his or her body in unison with the movement of the horse. Should a horse do something it should not like shying, bucking or rearing, they should be able to still go with it, and not leave by the shortest route at the first possible hint of trouble.

Don't though expect to be able to cope with a difficult horse before you have learnt to ride a calm, kind one first. This takes time. Gain your own confidence first and your balance and then you can progress to more lively rides.

Do remember it is as foolish to ride a horse too big for one, as it is to try and ride one that is not suitable in temperament. Both spell trouble.

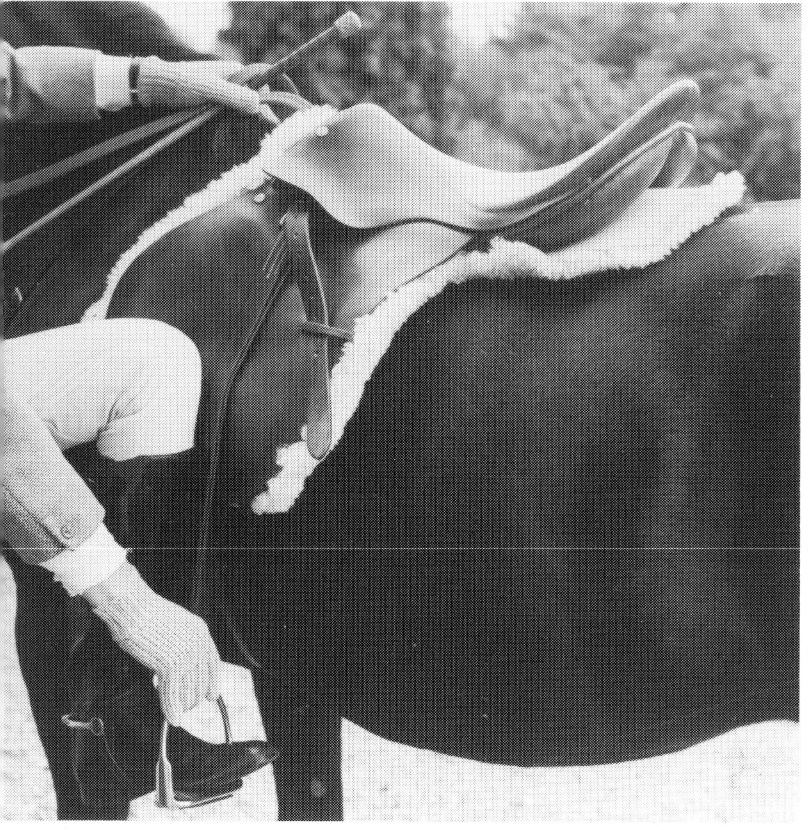

29. Mounting – place the toe of the left foot in the stirrup iron so that the weight falls on the ball of the foot; the left hand in the meantime holds both reins and the rider's stick and is placed on the withers to prevent the horse moving forward.

33. Next place the right hand right over the saddle and grip the edge of the far flap, and then with a spring from the right foot raise yourself into a standing position in the near-side stirrup iron and swing the right leg over the horse's back taking care not to either dig the horse in the tummy with the left toe or kick it on the back with the right; then lower yourself gently into the saddle and place the right foot in the off-side iron.

34. Dismounting – kick both feet free of the irons, take the reins in the left hand; then swinging one's weight forward over the withers, while at the same time swinging the right leg over the horse's back, slide gently to the ground alongside the horse's near-side shoulder.

Don't resent having to be led to start with or to having to ride in an enclosed space – this is the only safe way to learn.

Do remember when riding to hold your reins correctly and keep your hands an inch or two above the front of the saddle, in this way you will have better contact with your horse's mouth and therefore better control.

Don't when you start riding, ride for too long. This only leads to strained muscles.

Do remember to avoid kicking your horse on the quarters when you dismount, or job him in the mouth. It upsets even the most long suffering equines.

Don't forget to pat your horse when it has done something you have asked of it and when you finish a ride. It is the rider's way of saying thank you to the horse.

Do remember to loosen your girths and run up your stirrup irons once you have dismounted.

Don't take it for granted you own the road, always remember to thank motorists who slow down for you and show you consideration in other ways. Good relations between riders and motorists are essential.

Do remember when riding not to upset other people using the same paths or open ground. They have equal rights if in a public place, and if on private land, then you are the guest of the land owner. Never ride on private land without permission, nor leave gates open, ride over crops or through growing grass. Milking cows and other stock must be left undisturbed too.

Do remember to wear your cap or hard hat, and have the drawstring adjusted to give the essential inch clearance between skull and hat.

Don't wear a scarf under a cap – if you do the cap is too big.

Do remember to approach your horse quietly and from either the side or front, speaking to it as you do so.

Don't make any hasty movements, these startle even the quietest horse.

Do remember when mounting to keep your toe so it cannot dig into your horse; it will take it as a signal to move off and you require it to stand still.

Do remember to sit up straight, not stiff, but relaxed and well down in the saddle.

Don't curl up like a caterpillar, this only makes you insecure in the saddle and prevents you using your legs correctly.

Don't forget either the Highway Code or Country Code; nor take a high handed attitude with people who do not share your own enjoyment of riding. Just because you are on a horse does not make you any different from other people. Always remember good manners go a long way to good relations with one's fellow beings.

And lastly, do remember it is your horse who gives you all your pleasure, so treat him well and go to the trouble of discovering how he should be treated and cared for. Riding is the best sport in the world and opens many doors for the newcomer – young or old, any age can ride if they have a real wish to do so.

6. Riding as a pastime and sport

Once confidence has been gained and the rider feels at home walking and trotting in an enclosed space, and possibly cantering too, the time has been reached when rides can become more adventurous. The rider's muscles will have become accustomed to the new strain imposed on them and a proper ride will not tire them unduly.

Hacking – riding for pure pleasure, will for some be all they wish to do; for others it will be a relaxation and pleasure to be mixed in with other forms of riding. When one goes for a hack one in fact merely goes for a ride around open countryside, along bye-roads or, if one lives in the country and owns land, across the fields and through the woods. Drift roads and bridleways open many tracks of countryside to the ordinary rider. If possible avoid main roads, anyway until you are in complete control of your horse under all circumstances. If you must ride on roads keep well into the left hand side of the road and do not go to sleep or let your horse. It is dangerous to dream along as this is how accidents can and do happen.

Clothes for hacking need not be one's best, but should fit and be clean. A hard hat or cap is essential; boots with proper heels and either breeches or jodhpurs, though many do ride in jeans or trousers. But as I said in an earlier chapter these are not to be recommended. In summer an open neck shirt or pullover will be enough, but in winter an anorak or proper hacking jacket (tweed) will be necessary. For formal hacking, a collar and tie with a hacking jacket will be required. This is known as 'Rat catcher'. A short stick or flat ended whip (the fish tailed sort are excellent as they give a smack but cannot cut) is correct if you require a stick, and for the more experienced who have complete control of the movement of their legs, a pair of blunt, short necked spurs may be worn. No *Novice* should wear spurs though until they can ride, with full control. The neck of the spur is always worn downwards. Their object is to enhance the leg aids not to inflict pain. Mis-use is extremely cruel, and cruelty is something no true horseman or woman will tolerate for a second.

Pony trekking – a pastime enjoyed for the countryside it opens up to many who would not otherwise have the chance to enjoy it. Some people who go for a pony trekking holiday have never really ridden before. If possible, for their own sake and that of their horses, they should try and have a few lessons before setting off. Remember too, to have anti-tetanus injections (every rider should be protected against tetanus as cuts and scratches are only too easy to come by, and some districts are more prone to tetanus than others), and if you suffer from hay fever or other similar ailments take a supply of your usual drugs to combat the trouble, it will often be worse in the country than in a town.

Clothes required are similar to those used for hacking informally. Be comfortable, be warm enough or if very hot, cool enough. One word of warning, if you wear nylon underclothes, do not wear nylon next to your skin, cotton between nylon and you will prevent burning. Believe me this nylon burning can be very sore. Nylon sets up friction. Before deciding on a centre for your holiday, find out if the one you fancy is a registered centre and provides good horses and ponies well cared for. The 'Ponies of Britain Club' run an approved scheme and they will send you a list of places that should be all right. There are some very good centres and some that are pure hell for the horses and ponies, and should never be allowed to operate. Avoid the latter at all costs.

Sponsored rides – a popular way of raising money for charity. You have to ride anything from five to twenty miles at a stretch. Not for the pure novice but fun once you have control and are riding fit. Clothes are the same as for hacking.

Long distance riding – this is a branch of riding for the more advanced and a step beyond the sponsored ride stage. Well within the bounds of the ordinary rider once they can ride. Clothes the same as above; but for big competitions formal hacking clothes may be required. To embark on these rides one must be knowledge-able about the care of the horse as it is asking a lot of them.

Showing – competitive riding embraces many different types of classes. Ridden classes require the rider to be clean and neatly dressed. Black or blue cap (or bowler if prefered), hacking jacket, or black or blue coat and breeches and long boots. A shirt and collar and tie is correct in the ring, and the rider should carry a short stick and wear blunt spurs. Gloves are best in brown leather.

Dressage – Black or blue coat, hunting stock (a collar and tie is permissible on some occasions in the summer), black or blue cap and pale breeches and top boots. Sticks are allowed in some tests but not others, and spurs are optional in tests up to a certain grade. Read all the rules and then carry them out.

Show-jumping – either rat-catcher, or a black, blue or red coat with a hard hat is usual for those not in the Forces; they can ride big competitions in uniform. White ties are now permitted in place of white stocks.

Eventing – a sport that embraces three different branches of riding, each requiring different clothes. *Dressage* requires a black coat with a hunting stock and either a cap, bowler or silk hat, or else uniform; *Show-jumping* for which the same clothes as dressage are needed, but the rider may carry a stick; and *Cross-country* for which the coat and cap are changed in favour of either a polo-necked sweater or shirt (plain – not fancy), and a proper crash skull with cover. Fancy clothes have no place in competitive riding. *Long Distance Riding, Dressage* and *Eventing* require the rider to belong to the B.H.S., while for *Show-Jumping* they must belong to the B.S.J.A. if they wish to compete at official shows and events. The horse too, must be registered in accordance with the rules governing the sport concerned.

Hunting – a sport enjoyed by many and which calls on the riders to be able to ride across country without knowing what they are going to jump. During the autumn Cub-hunting takes place in the early morning when the young hounds are taught how to hunt. Mounted followers can come out if they ask and should wear Rat-catcher. (Tweed coat, collar and tie and breeches with long boots.) Always be clean and tidy. It is customary to carry a hunting whip to open gates and ward-off hounds from your horse's legs to prevent hounds getting kicked. Once the Opening Meet arrives (November) it is usual to change one's tweed coat for either a black one or Hunt coat, and one's collar and tie for a hunting stock (white). A sweater is changed in the case of a Hunt coat for a waistcoat. Hunting caps are really only worn by the Master, Hunt Servants, farmers and a few special followers, but now many women wear them with a black or blue coat (a silk hat is worn with a side-saddle habit), and providing the Master has no objection, they have become permissible. Nevertheless, when going to a new Hunt or starting to hunt it is polite to ask the Hunt Secretary if it is all right to wear one. Men should wear a bowler or silk hat with a black coat – depending on its cut, and a silk hat with a Hunt coat, pink (scarlet) in most hunts with a special collar, but a few hunts like The Duke of Beaufort's wear a different colour, in their case 'The Blue and Buff'. A Hunt coat may only be worn by those who have been invited to wear one, the same applies to the Hunt Button. The Hunt Staff normally wear the same coats as the members of the Hunt, but a few like the Duke of Beaufort's, Heythrop and Berkeley, have different coats – green in the case of the first two, and musk (deep yellow) for the latter. Harriers too, wear green coats. Though black boots are correct with an ordinary black coat, mahogany tops (deep brown or a series of shades to very pale, according to fancy) are correct with a Hunt coat. White breeches and boot straps accompany these, whereas buff or pale breeches are correct with an ordinary hunting coat. When hunting dress is called for in other sports, then one of the above is what is required. If you wish to hunt, write to your local Hunt Secretary. He will then tell you the subscription etc. Owing to the large numbers who now hunt, some Hunts are forced to limit the number of visitors from outside their own hunt, so you may find a few restrictions concerning the horse you ride – it may have to be stabled within the Hunt, etc. Nevertheless, many smaller Hunts can still welcome people who do not live in their area and these Hunts will give the newcomer just as much fun and pleasure as the large Hunts. If you live in a hunting district, then there should be no problem. The restrictions are necessary for the sake of the land over which they hunt. Remember, when out hunting you are the guest of the Master and landowners, so refrain from jumping fences unnecessarily and going off to enjoy yourself where you have no business to be. The Field Master is there to control the field (mounted followers), so if he asks you to stay somewhere, or go somewhere else, do so. The day's sport depends very largely on the field behaving itself in a sensible and considerate manner. For the newcomer to the sport, the B.H.S. has a very useful booklet *Riding to Hounds*, which will give a good insight into what a day's hunting is all about.

Hunter Trials – a cross-country event in which a rider rides a natural, or near natural, stretch of country. It is very similar to the cross-country section of an event. The clothes required are rat-catcher, ordinary hunting coat or a Hunt coat. Some riders now favour a crash scull and sweater, which in the case of Trials not run as a Hunt function is perfectly acceptable. Some are wise and wear a crash scull and dark cover with a coat. The main thing is to be neat, clean and tidy.

Wet weather riding calls for a mackintosh with proper leg straps to prevent the flaps flying up; whereas cold weather riding requires very warm underclothes. Thick, heavy duty plain nylon tights are excellent under nylon breeches or jodhpurs providing one has either cotton or wool pants on underneath them, next to one's skin.

So much for some of the many forms of riding open to one once the plunge has been taken to start. How much one rides or to what standard depends on the rider – they can go as far or not as they wish.

Riding brings endless pleasure to many throughout the world – both fit, able bodied people and those whose bodies have not their full power, so I hope this booklet will have opened the doors to those who have yet to find what enjoyment awaits them.

THE BRITISH HORSE SOCIETY
National Equestrian Centre, Stoneleigh, Kenilworth, Warwickshire.

THE PONIES OF BRITAIN CLUB,
Brookside Farm, Ascot, Berks.